ABCs

ONE LETTER EACH PAGE

Noah's Ark

Bible COLORING
Dot Markers Activity Book

With BIG DOT Circles

★ Black reverse pages for less bleed-through! ★ AGES 2+ ★

This book is made to be used with paint daubers or dot markers. Each page has a black background on the reverse to help with bleed-through. Also, you can cut out each page using the trim line or use a separate piece of paper between pages. Have fun!

Adam and Apple

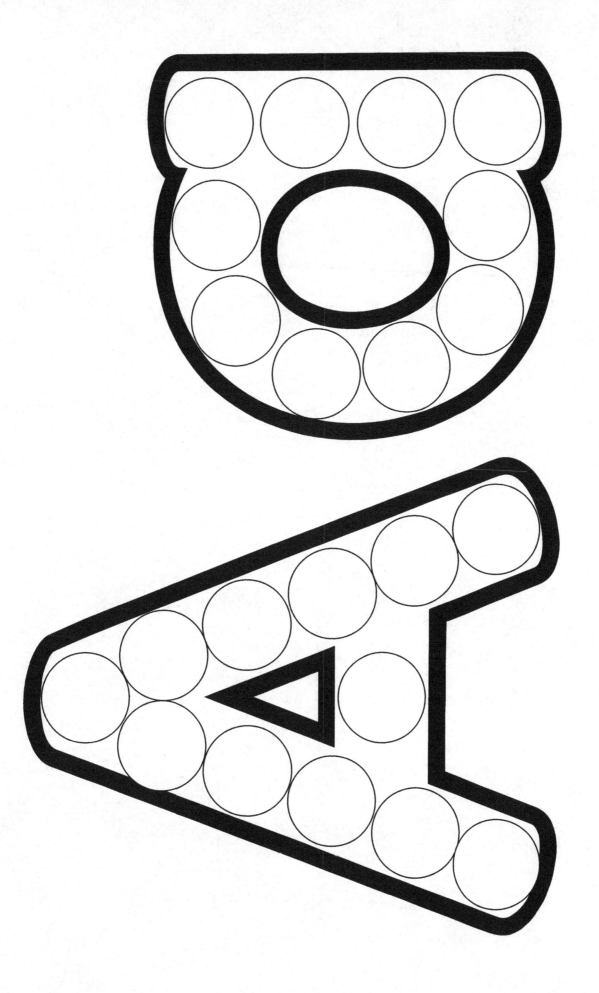

Bible

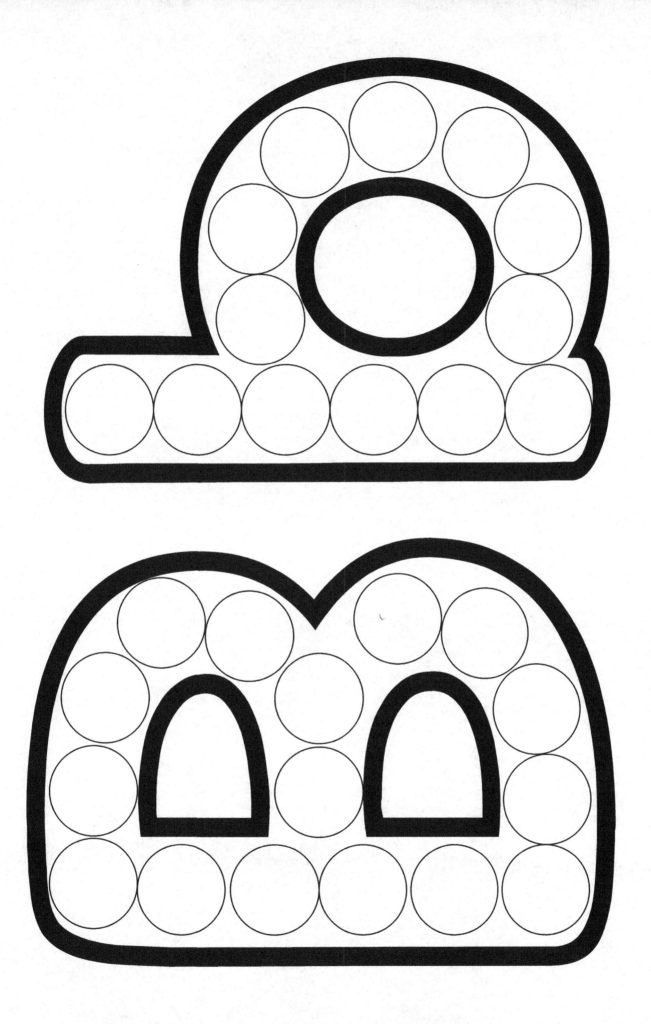

Cross

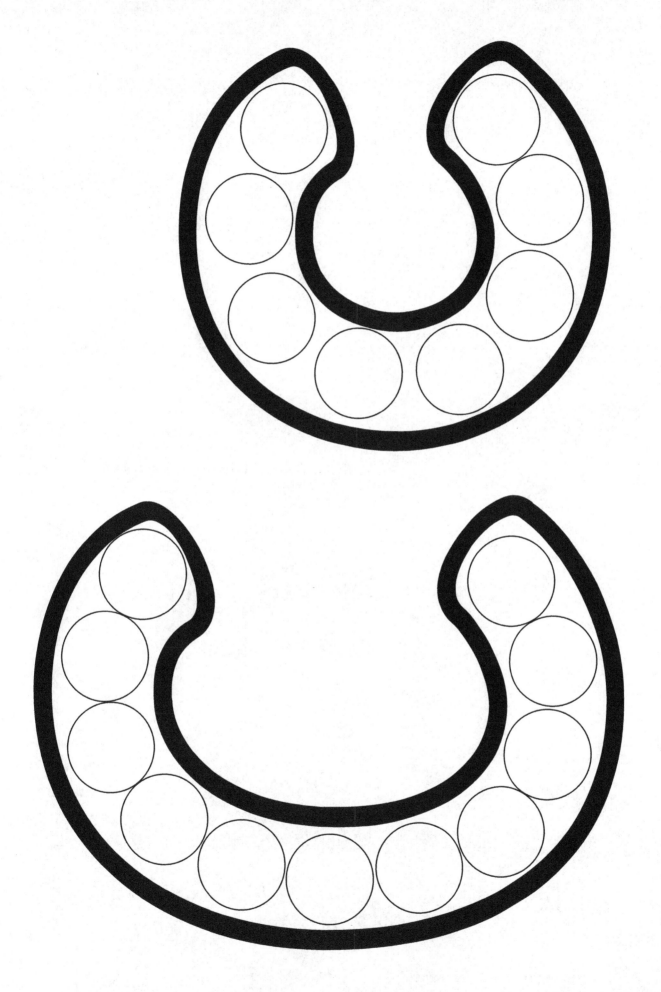

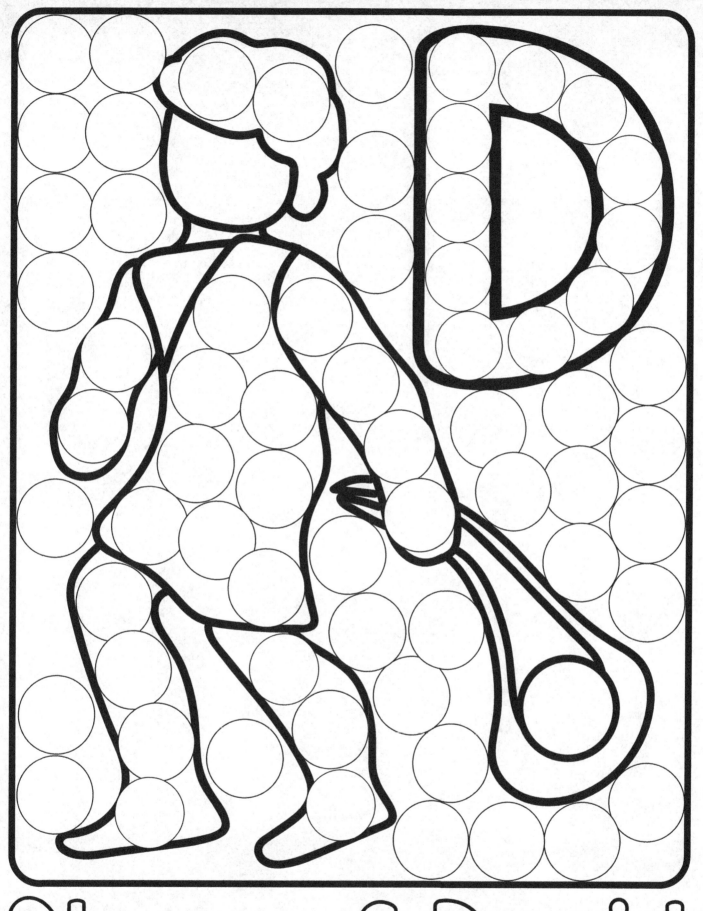

Story of David

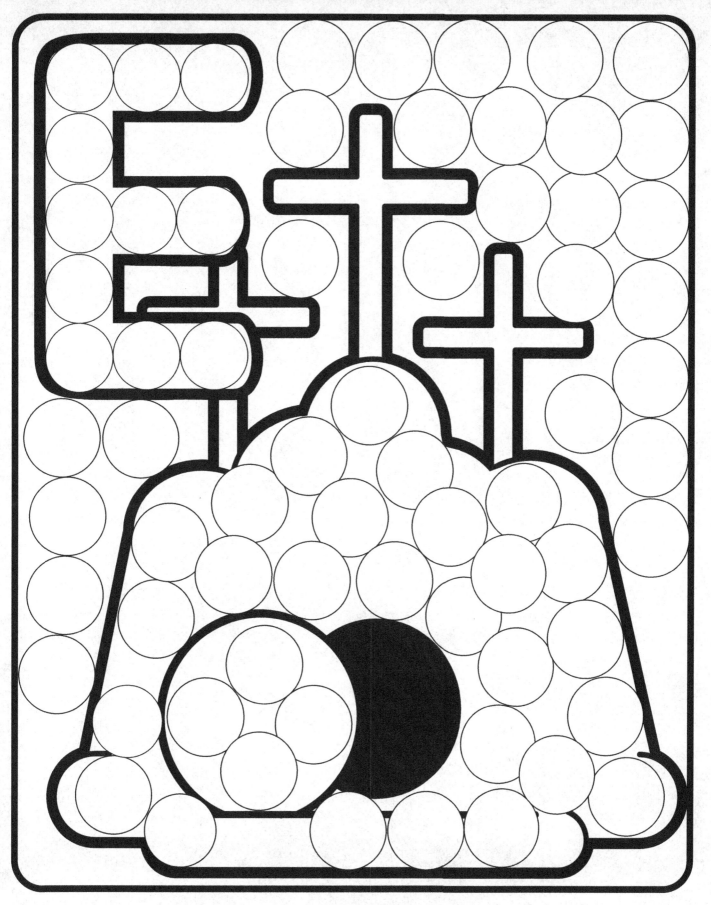

Easter

Fish

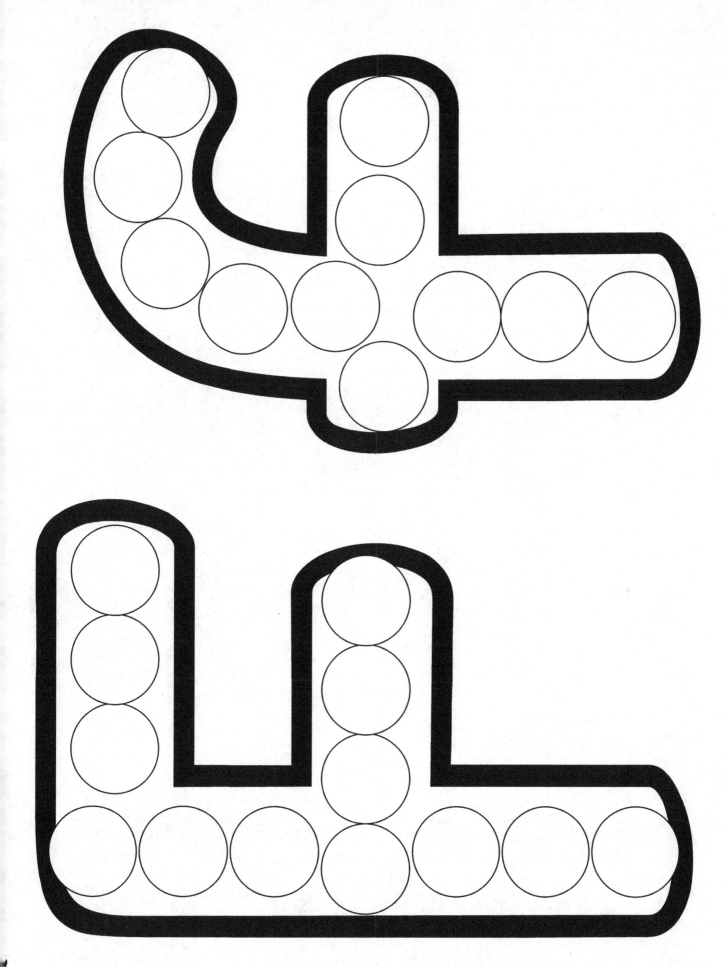

God's Earth

Heaven

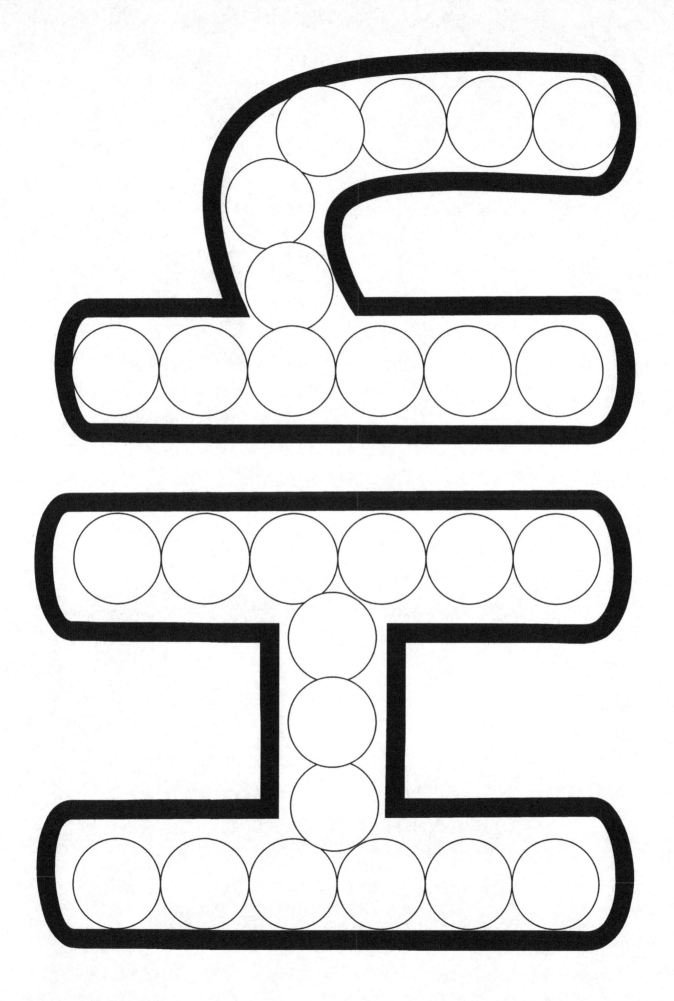

Israel

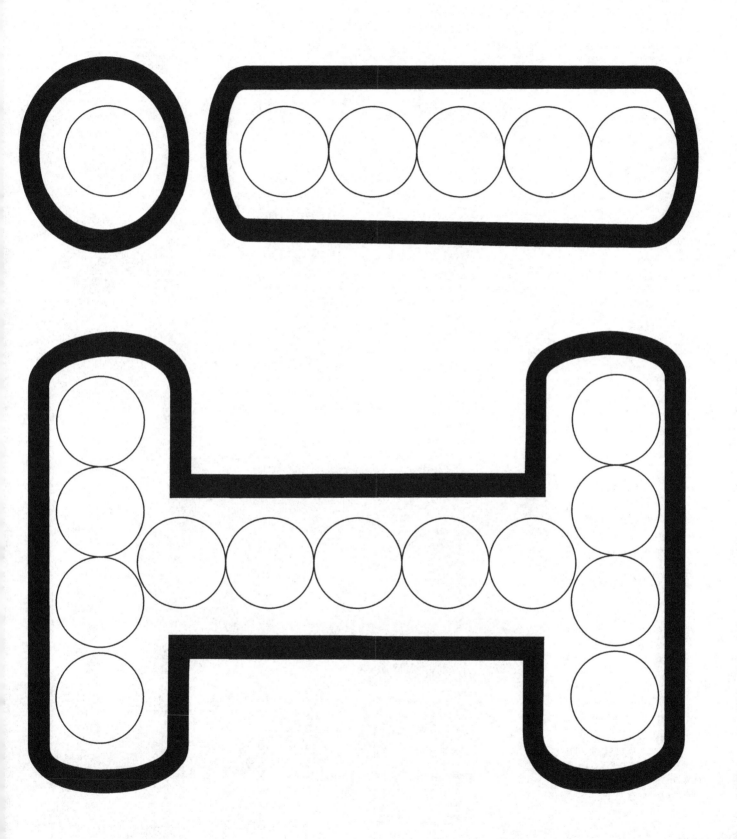

Jesus

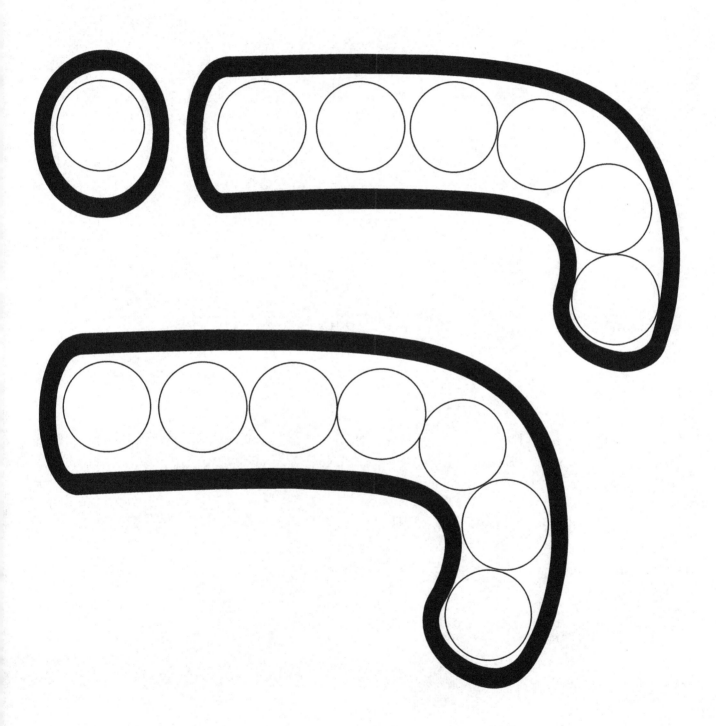

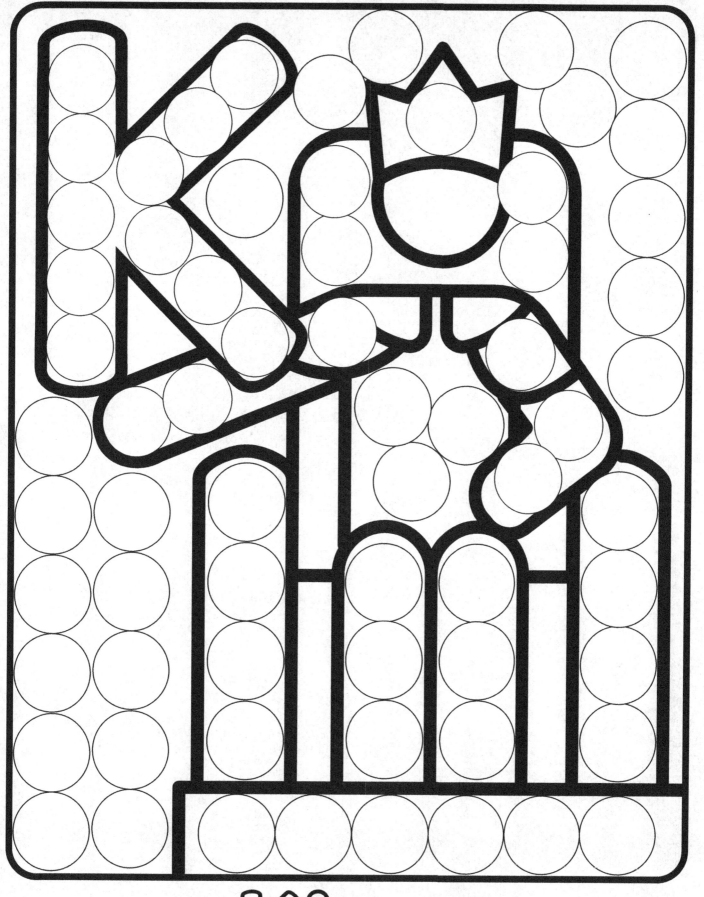

King

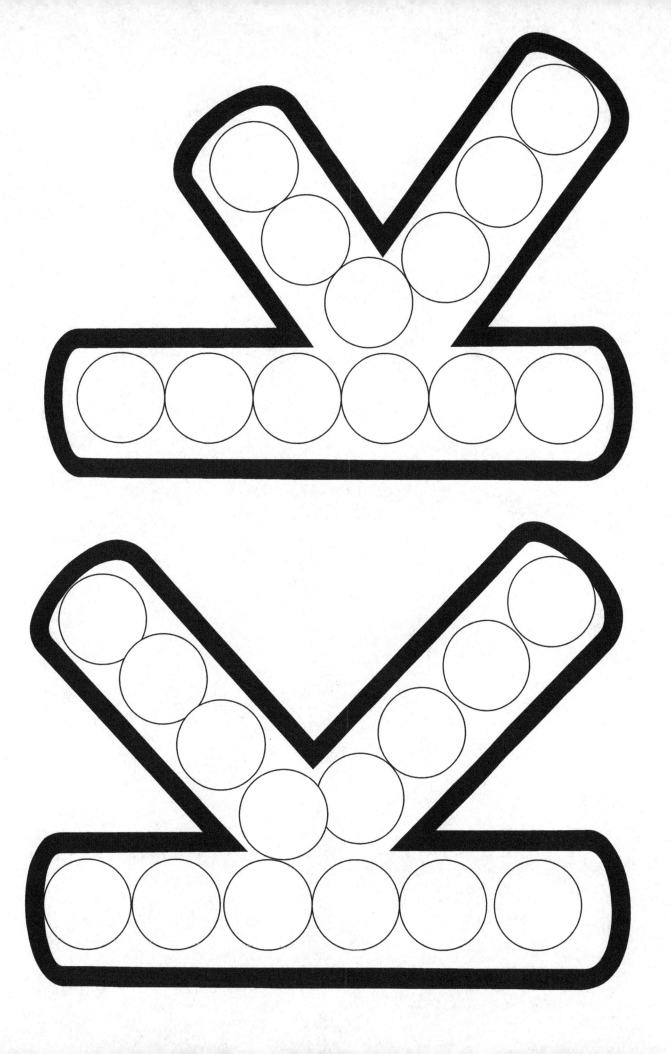

Lamb

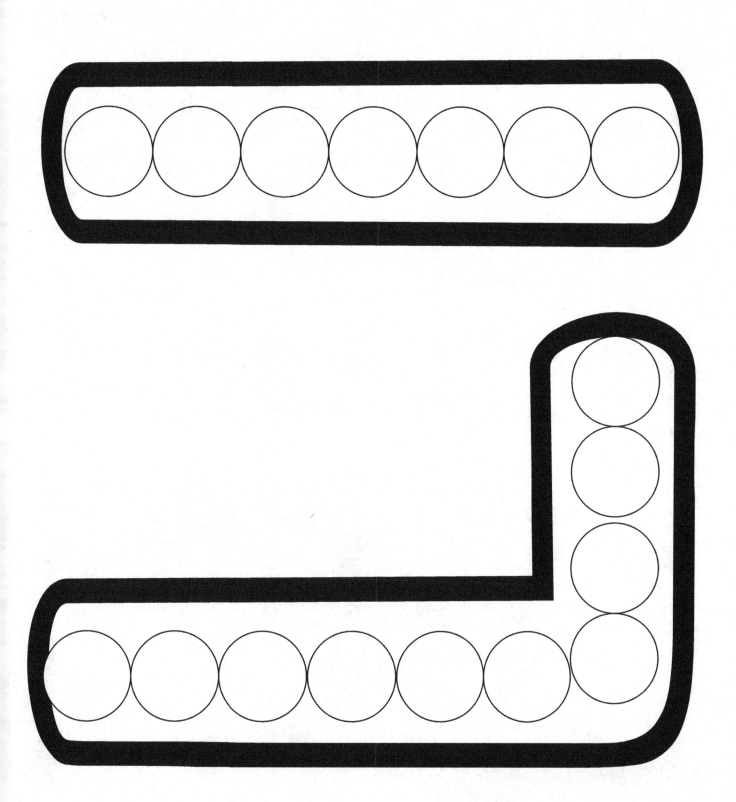

Moses

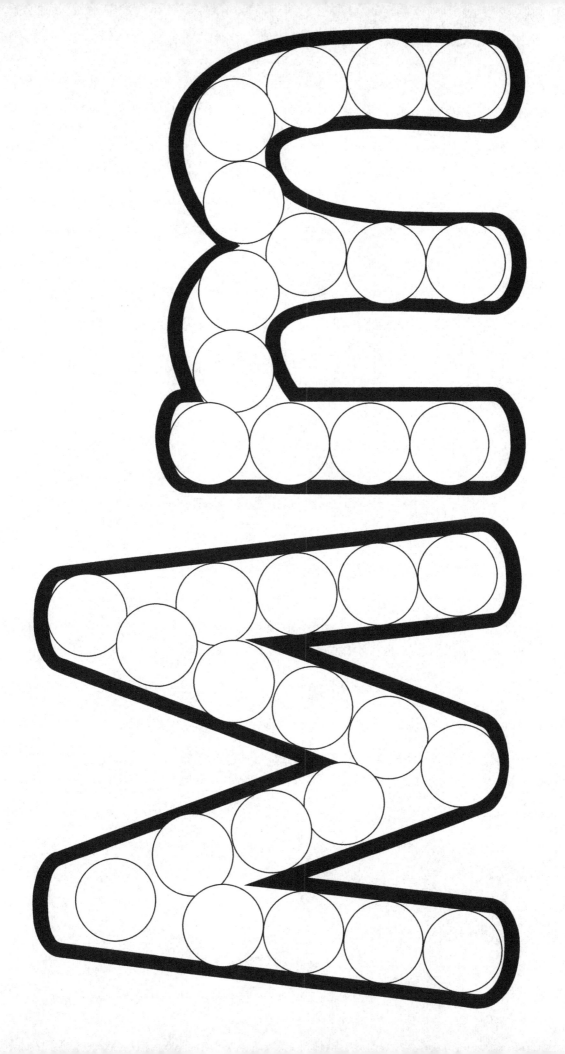

Noah's Ark

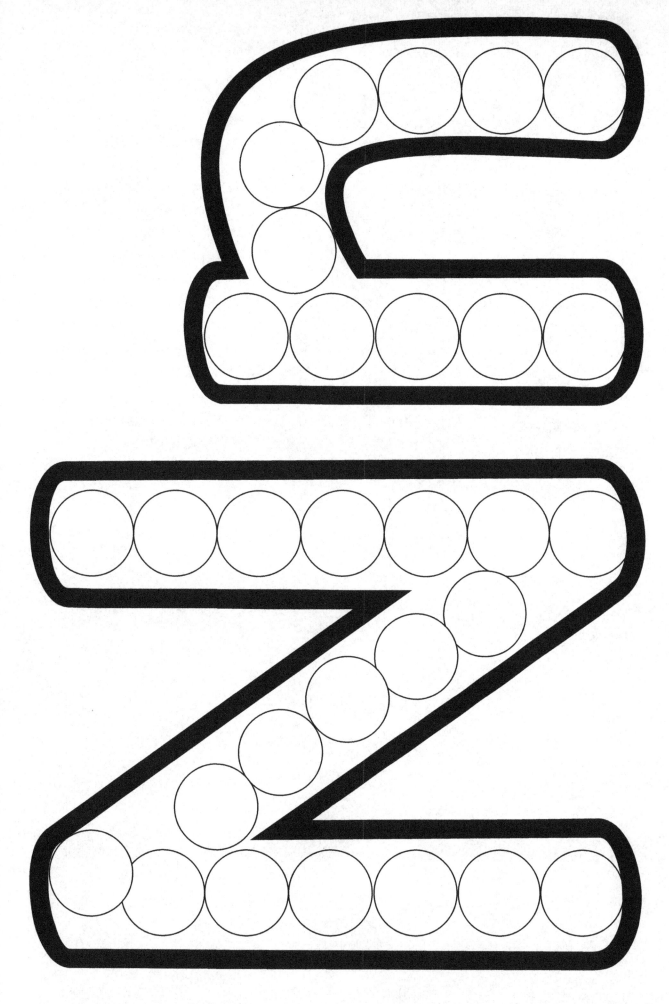

Olive Branch

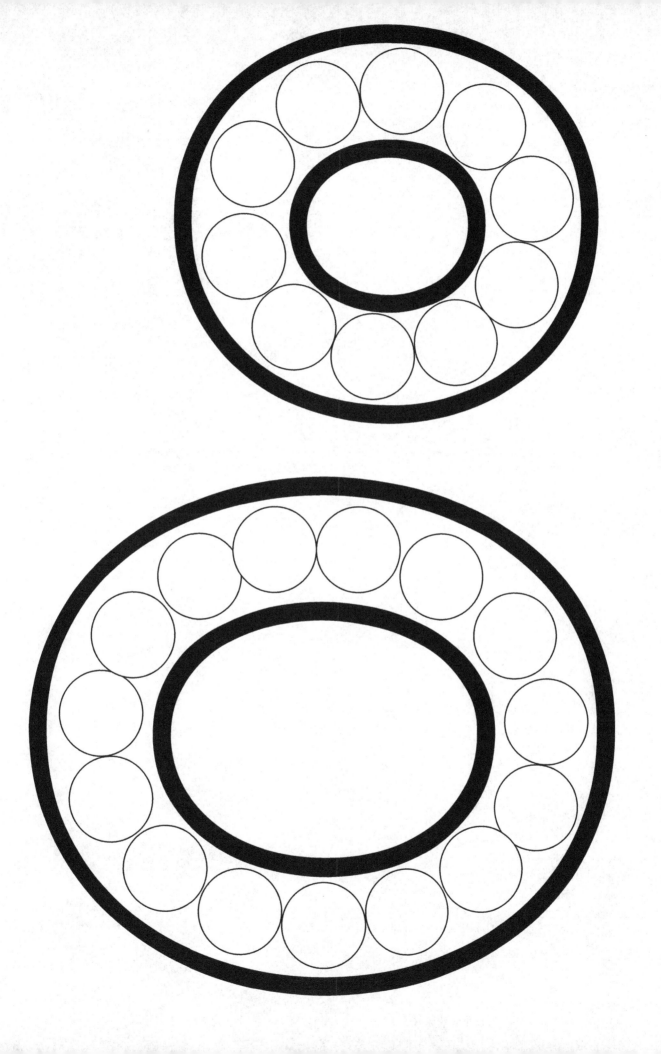

Pray

Queen Esther

Rainbow

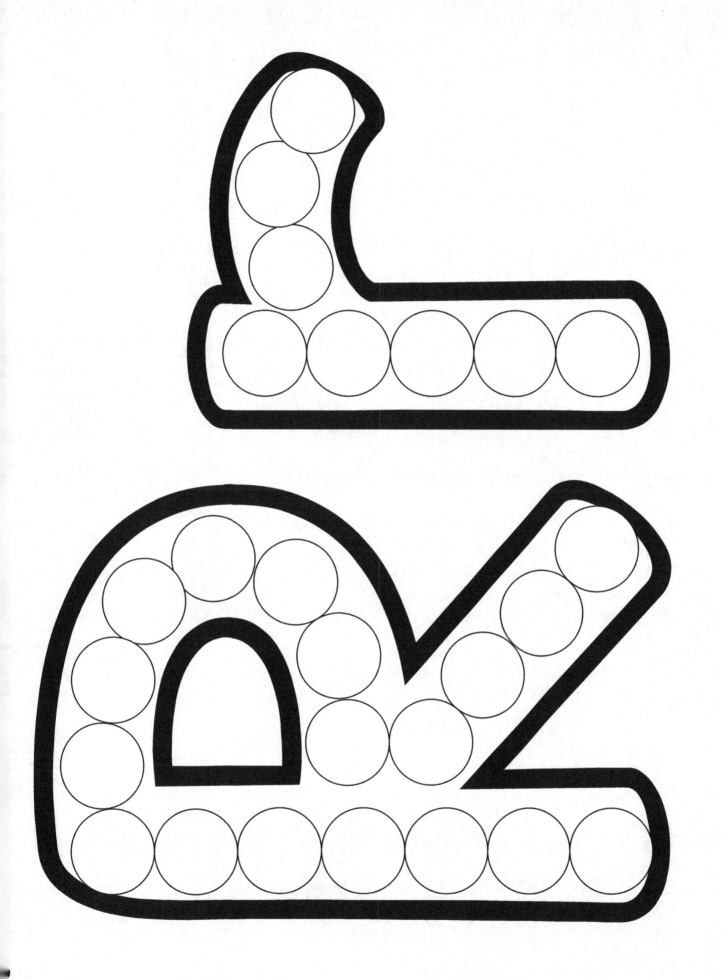

Savior

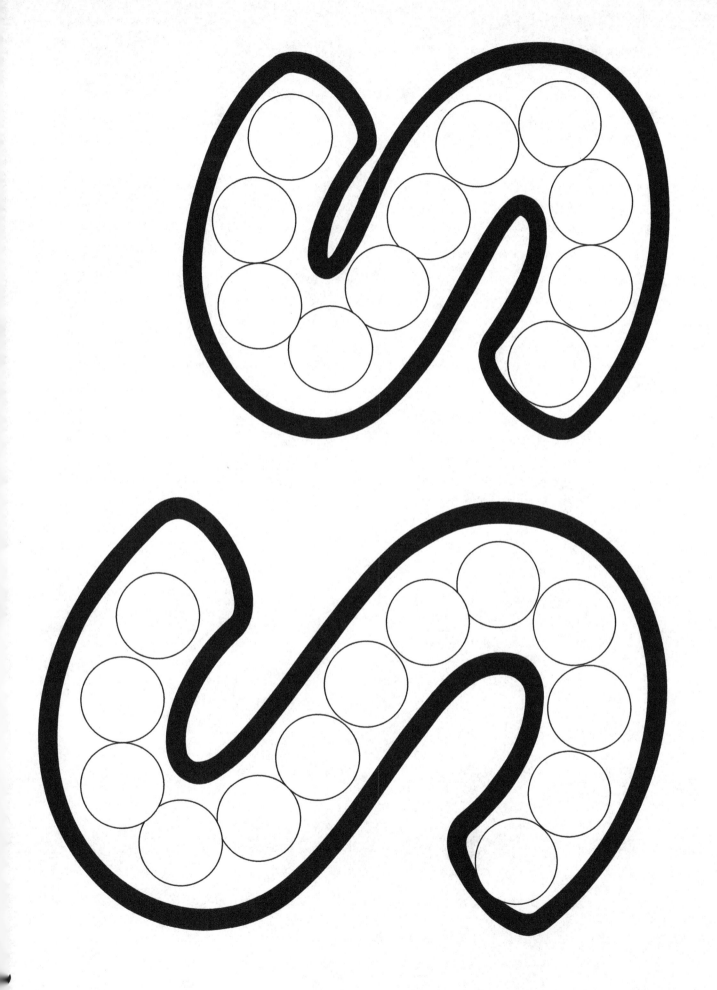

Trinity

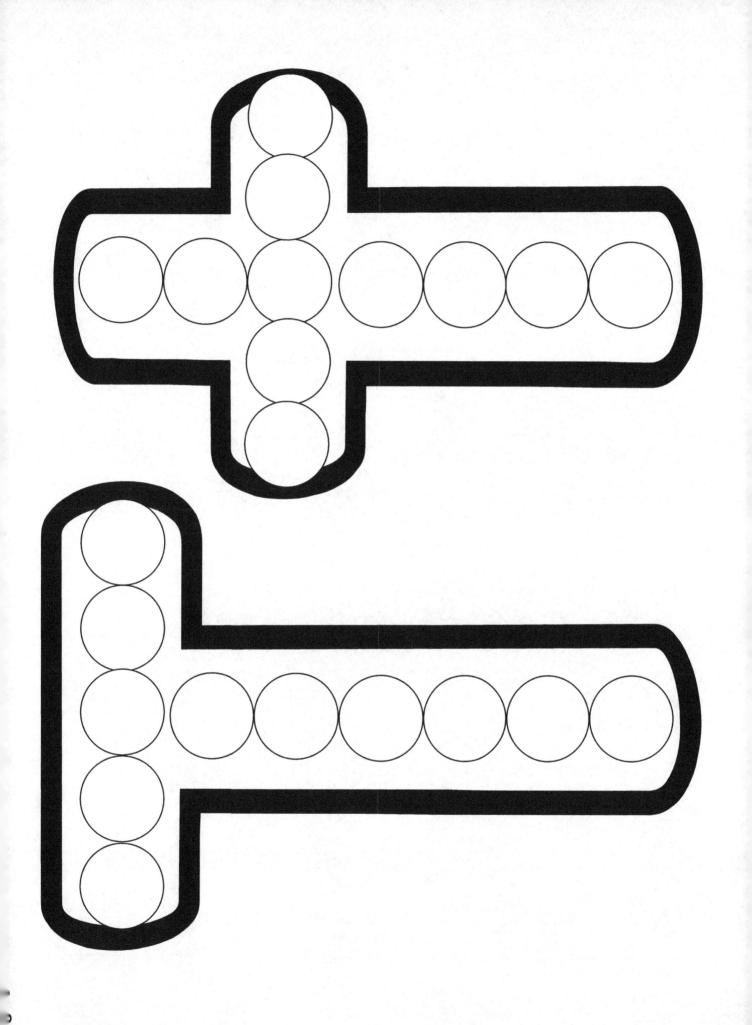

Unity

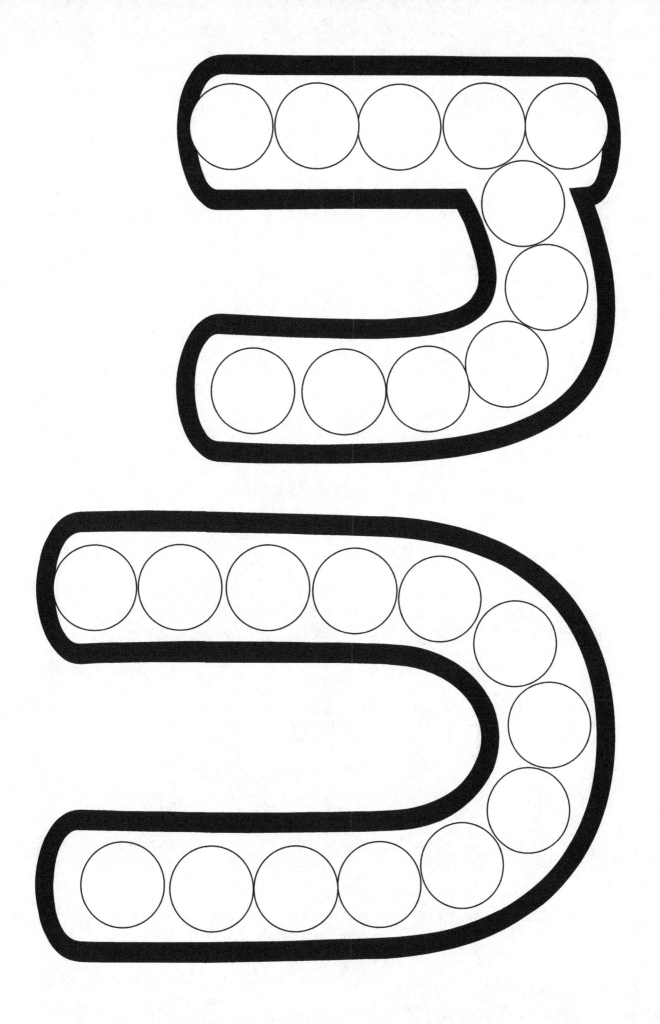

Vine

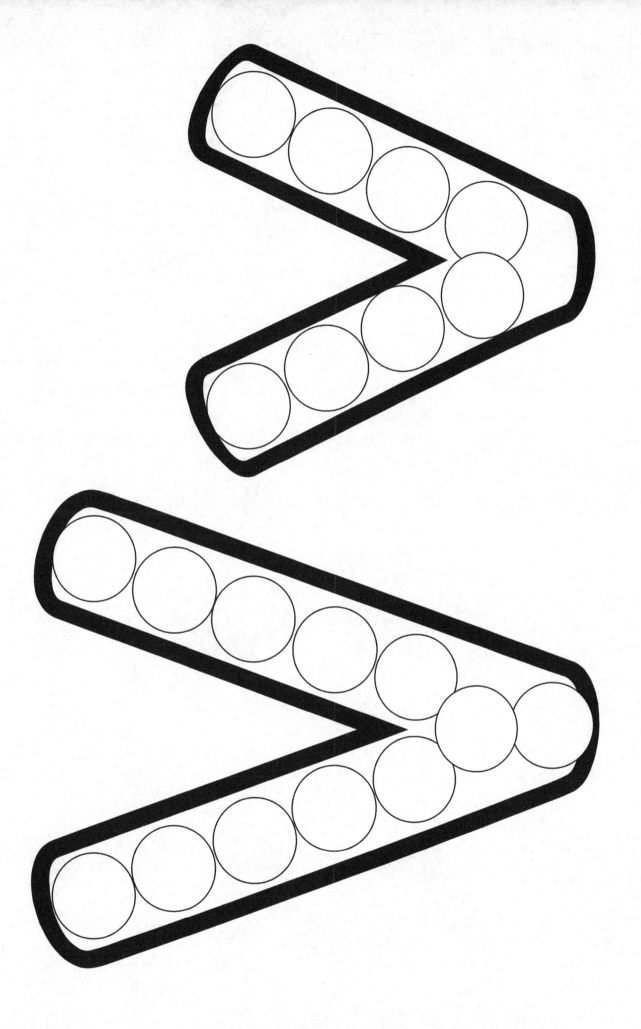

Jonah and the Whale

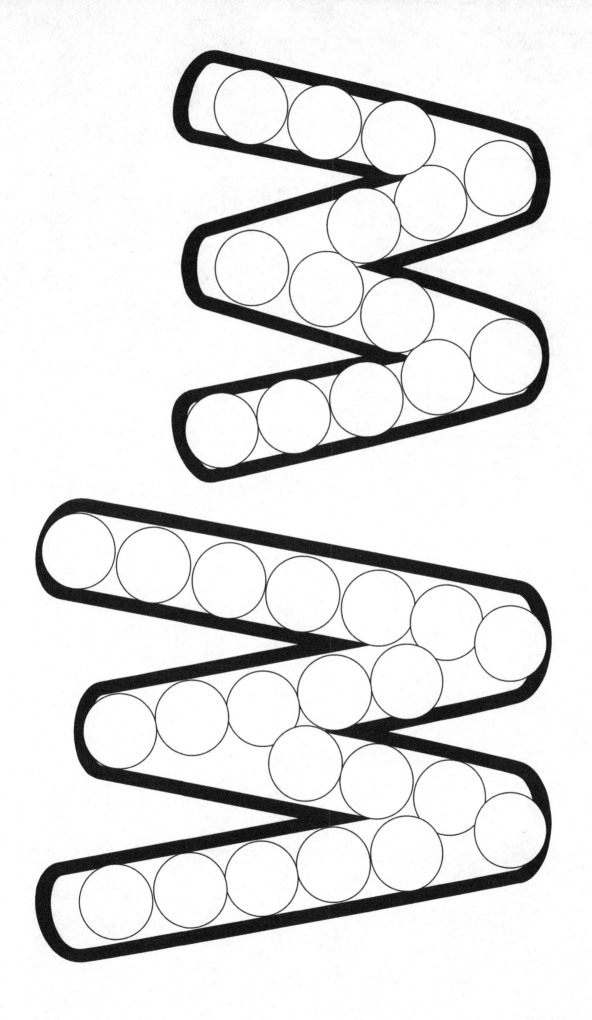

Crucifix

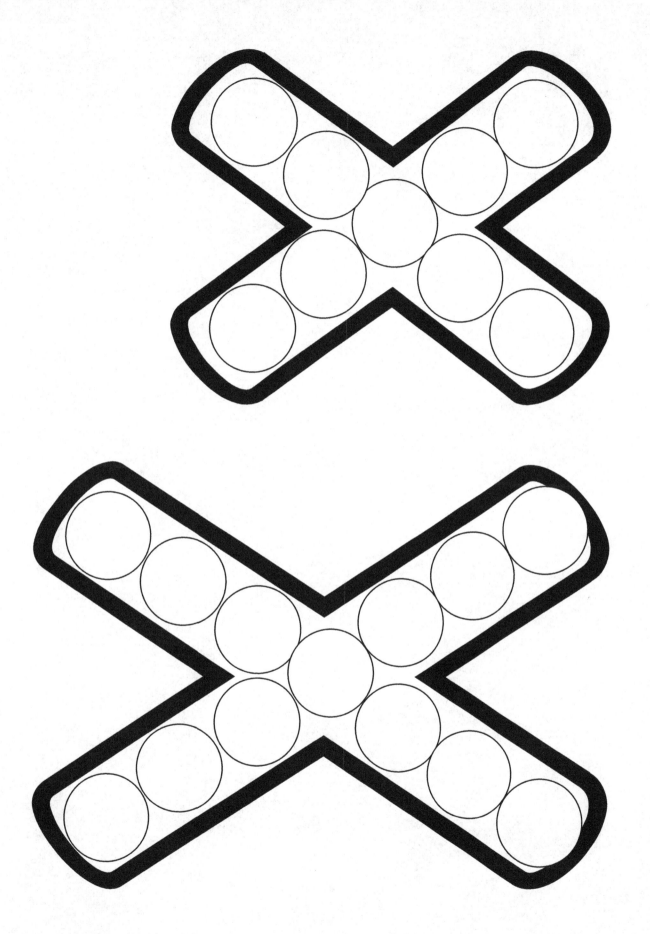

Yahweh

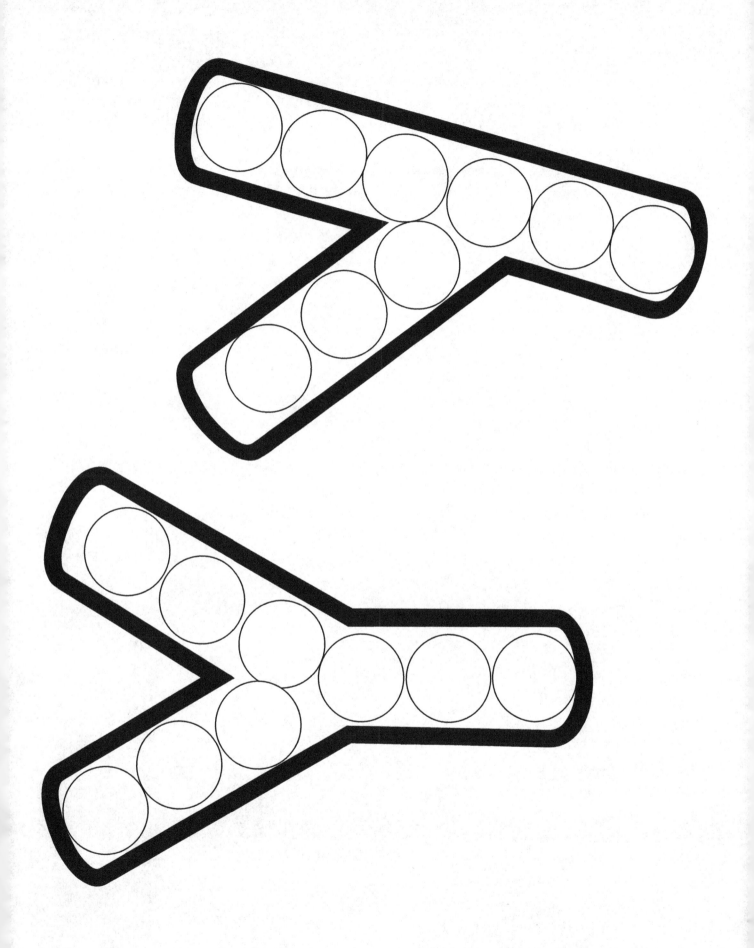

Zion

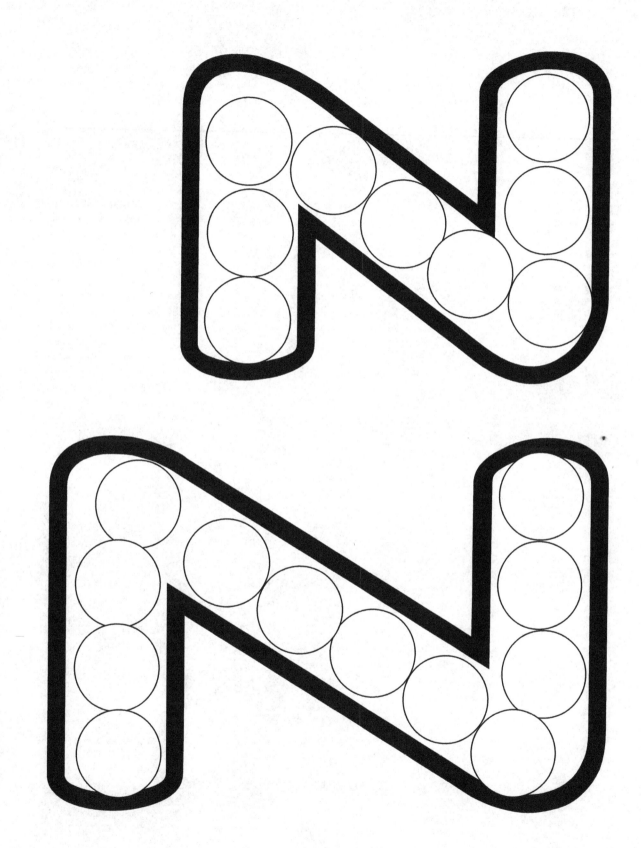